ONE STAR WONDERS

Also by Mike Lowery

Bug Scouts Camp Out

Bug Scouts Out in the Wild

Everything Awesome About Dinosaurs

Everything Awesome About Sharks

Everything Awesome About Space

Random Illustrated Facts: A Collection of Curious, Weird, and Totally Not Boring Things to Know

★☆☆☆

Andrews McMeel Publishing
a division of Andrews McMeel Universal
1130 Walnut Street, Kansas City, Missouri 64106

www.andrewsmcmeel.com

23 24 25 26 27 SDB 10 9 8 7 6 5 4 3 2 1

ISBN: 978-1-5248-7498-8

Library of Congress Control Number: 2022948900

Editor: Patty Rice
Art Director/Designer: Diane Marsh
Production Editor: Jasmine Lim
Production Manager: Tamara Haus

ATTENTION: SCHOOLS AND BUSINESSES
Andrews McMeel books are available at quantity discounts with bulk purchase for educational, business, or sales promotional use. For information, please e-mail the Andrews McMeel Publishing Special Sales Department: sales@amuniversal.com.

★★★★★

ONE STAR
WONDERS

THE (WORST) REVIEWS
of the WORLD'S
GREATEST PLACES

COLLECTED and ILLUSTRATED By

MIKE LOWERY

Andrews McMeel
PUBLISHING®

I ALMOST SKIPPED
THE TAJ MAHAL.

A few years ago, I was finally able to visit a destination that had long been at the top of my travel list: India. The problem was I only had one week to explore the massive country. I knew I wouldn't be able to see it all, but I wanted to pack in as much as possible. I hoped to see a few top sights and still somehow leave feeling like I'd seen the *real* India. So, I sat and researched. I looked at itineraries suggested in books and online and started making notes.

No matter how deep I dug, every list, article, and guide I read included one thing: the Taj Mahal. Of course they did. For some, just the name is enough to spark wanderlust. It's a bucket list item many have promised themselves to see before they die. I guess it's assumed that if you've made it to New Delhi, you're going to make the easy ride down to Agra to see one of the Seven Wonders of the Modern World.

But, wait. How could I be POSITIVE that I wanted to go? How does anyone know what movies to see, what local restaurants to try, or which inflatable air mattresses to buy online? That's right! I looked up the reviews. Did you know that you could review a landmark? Were you aware that anyone on the planet can write their thoughts down for an entire city or even a country?

★☆☆☆☆

And how were the reviews for the Taj Mahal? They were (mostly) great. I read through the more than 30,000 reviews on one site alone and found phrases like "It took my breath away!" and "Absolutely stunning." Some visitors wept. Some asked their partners for their hand in marriage in its shadow. Post after post gave this spot the highest reward a review site can give, FIVE STARS.

I didn't stay long in the five-star section, however. The constant gushing is boring. The praise is expected. Instead, I did what I'd done for years. I skipped down to the online travel world's weird and grimy underbelly. I scrolled to the one-star reviews.

What did user @MARK_BASSguy81 think of this nearly 400-year-old monument?

THE WIFI IS AWFUL! ONE STAR.

THE WONDERFUL WORLD
OF ONE-STAR REVIEWS.

For over a decade, I've collected one-star reviews like this one. I started with the ones of famous landmarks but slowly started collecting them for must-see places and films and for must-read books like *Moby Dick*. I find them funny and odd and am fascinated with how they often give more insight into the world of the review*er* than the review*ed*.

There are five major categories for negative reviews.

1. DISORGANIZATION – The tour group or company that runs the landmark is organized poorly and mismanages the visitors. These reviews often clearly state that the actual landmark is stunning, but the long, slow lines, non-refundable tickets, or something similar ruined the experience. Thankfully, these tend to be the majority of bad reviews of famous locations.

2. BAD PERSONAL EXPERIENCE – Again, the location was great, but something happened explicitly to the reviewer that made the visit unpleasant. This could be bad traffic, a lost personal item, or even not making it to the site at all. You'd be surprised to learn that many one-star reviews tend to include the phrase, "I never got to see it."

3. NOT HYPE-WORTHY – In these reviews, the visitor made it all the way to the location only to be perplexed by having heard about it their whole lives. It's just a centuries-old castle. It's simply a marble statue carved by hand. Why all the fuss? Reviewers in this category often have "Paris Syndrome," a type of depression that can set in after visiting a place you've idealized only to discover it's not as magical as you'd dreamt. Like, say, Paris, for example.

4. OOPS – This category, which happens way more than you think, is for reviews made by users who clearly don't understand that five stars are good and one star is bad. These tend to be the ones I laugh out loud at most consistently. They usually go something like, "We absolutely loved it! ONE STAR!"

I've titled this last category with the most common phrase in the history of travel-related one-star reviews. These two simple words can deter even the most avid traveler.

5. TOO TOURISTY – This category is the one I find the most intriguing and identify with the most. It's the result of our desire to see one of the most recognizable things on the planet and yet somehow be the only one who knows it exists. We want unobstructed views of the Sphinx. We want the Eiffel Tower all to ourselves. We want the ability to recreate the photo we saw on Instagram of the Blue Lagoon in Iceland. These reviewers are surprised to find it crowded at the Colosseum and shocked to see that vendors are selling T-shirts of the Mona Lisa in front of the Louvre. Who would've guessed?

There were reviews like these for the Taj Mahal. But something weird happened. I read them initially out of curiosity and then slowly got sucked in and started to worry that I would genuinely hate my experience if I went. The reviews led me to feel that this one excursion could have the power to ruin the entire trip.

WHAT DID I DO?

After a few days of debating, I went with the guidebooks and my intuition and visited the Taj Mahal. It was crowded, and the lines were long. Vendors pulled on me to look at crummy keychains and magnets. Tourists blocked the best views and posed, pretending to hold the building up using forced perspective.

And I loved it. It didn't change my life in the way that the trip as a whole did, but I saw a beautiful building with a long, rich history. What was my review? I didn't write one because I'm not an insane person who reviews landmarks.

★☆☆☆☆

This book is a collection of illustrated one-star reviews inspired by some of my favorites that I've read over the years. It's sort of like the opposite of a travel guide.

—MIKE

TAJ MAHAL

Agra, India

★☆☆☆☆

"If you like crowds, you'll love this place."

ULURU
(AYERS ROCK)

Australia

★☆☆☆☆

"We got snacks but they didn't give us plates or toothpicks."

TUSCANY

Tuscany, Italy

"We are a group that enjoys wine. The guy, Robert, said our entire
table couldn't have more wine. He said it in front of everybody."

ANTARCTICA

Antarctica

"Only had an hour for lunch."

SACRÉ COEUR

Paris, France

★☆☆☆☆

"Please, please, PLEASE do not go here."

BLUE LAGOON

Iceland

★☆☆☆☆

*"Went during a cyclone and the weather was terrible.
Someone stole my slippers."*

CATACOMBS OF PARIS

Paris, France

*"They didn't let us skip the line
even though my wife is pregnant."*

BESAKIH TEMPLE

Bali, Indonesia

★☆☆☆☆

*"Wow! Just wow! Amazing!
ONE STAR."*

KŌTOKU-IN,
THE GREAT BUDDHA
OF KAMAKURA

Kamakura, Japan

★☆☆☆☆

"It's old but not that 'great.'
More like 'ok-ish.'"

ROAD TO HANA

Maui, Hawai'i

"A three hour, nonstop, treacherous drive to nowhere."

ALASKA GLACIER TOUR

Alaska, USA

★☆☆☆☆

"Better and cheaper to watch online."

CENTRAL PARK

New York, USA

★☆☆☆☆

"NOT GREAT. A squirrel stole my hot dog and school children laughed at me."

CHICHÉN ITZÁ

Yucatán, Mexico

★☆☆☆☆

"The vendors make jaguar sounds."

GREAT WALL

China

★☆☆☆☆

"Just a pile of sloppily laid bricks."

ROCK OF GIBRALTAR

Gibraltar

"We were met with extreme hostility from the monkeys."

★☆☆☆☆

LAS VEGAS STRIP

Nevada, USA

"Five barf emojis."

HAGIA SOPHIA
GRAND MOSQUE

Istanbul, Turkey

★☆☆☆☆

"Free to get in, which is too expensive."

MOUNT FUJI

Japan

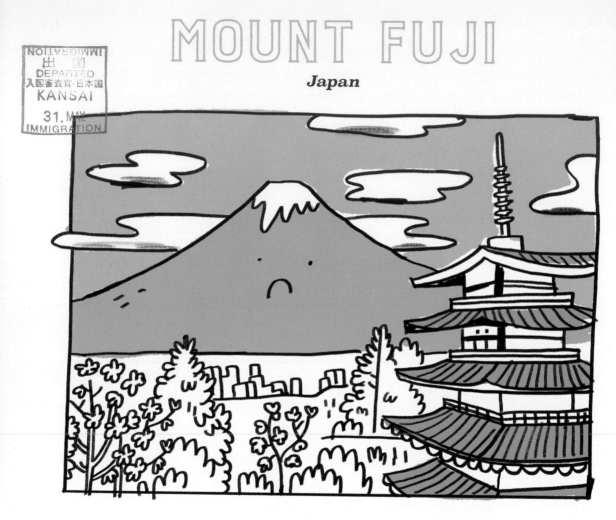

★☆☆☆☆

"I found it just ok."

BOOK OF KELLS

Dublin, Ireland

★☆☆☆☆

*"9 Euros to go in and look at an old book. There were
like people weeping over the books and whatnot—
too much for me. It was super boring."*

MOUNT KILIMANJARO

Tanzania

*"I asked my guide to stop hiking and go back
and he offered me a Red Bull."*

BASÍLICA DE LA SAGRADA FAMÍLIA

Barcelona, Spain

★☆☆☆☆

"A concrete monster in the middle of a beautiful city."

GREAT BARRIER REEF

Australia

★☆☆☆☆

*"The ocean was so rough that
everyone was vomiting."*

SYDNEY OPERA HOUSE

Sydney, Australia

★☆☆☆☆

"No light show. Don't believe what the 'WEBSITE' says.
THERE. WAS. NO. LIGHT. SHOW."

SANTORINI

Santorini, Greece

"Only ok for people who have never seen anything nice."

EASTER ISLAND

Chile

★☆☆☆☆

*"Avoid going if that psycho
park guard (Felipe) is still around."*

EIFFEL TOWER

Paris, France

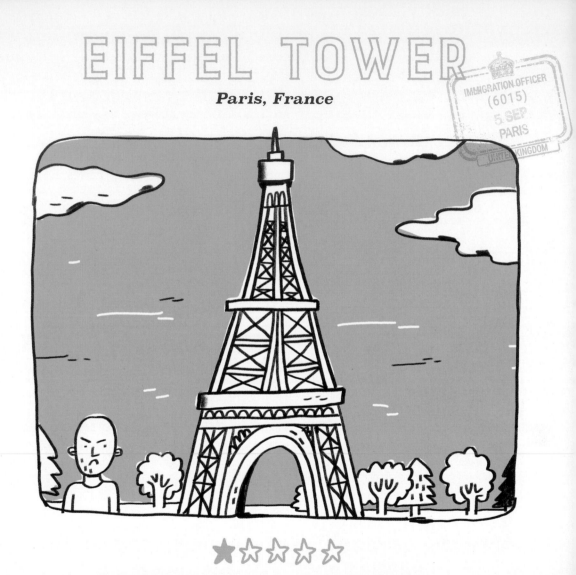

★☆☆☆☆

"Stupid tower, it doesn't do anything."

TATACOA DESERT

Colombia

"Just a rather uninteresting piece of land. Not much to do."

★☆☆☆☆

THE LITTLE
MERMAID STATUE

Copenhagen, Denmark

"The stinky little sculpture isn't even all that well-crafted and so tiny it feels like they ran out of bronze at the factory."

BILTMORE ESTATES

North Carolina, USA

★☆☆☆☆

"NEVER BEEN THERE."

WAITOMO
GLOWWORM CAVE

New Zealand

"They wouldn't let us in without tickets."

BIG BEN

London, England

★☆☆☆☆

"I had seen it before. Is it good for couples? No."

ANGKOR WAT

Krong Siem Reap, Cambodia

★☆☆☆☆

"The floors were uneven and a tripping hazard.
Just download photos from the web and enjoy your sleep."

TAHITI

French Polynesia

★☆☆☆☆

"I would say skip it. Around the world for nothing."

BRAN CASTLE

Transylvania, Romania

★☆☆☆☆

*"They told me you're not allowed to say
blah blah like a vampire on the tour."*

GOLDEN GATE BRIDGE

California, USA

"Just a bridge. There are so many wonderful and unique bridges in the world and this is not one of them."

PETRA

Jordan

★☆☆☆☆

"I saw a camel biting someone."

AMSTERDAM

Amsterdam, Netherlands

"Nothing special. LOTS of bikes!"

CAMINO DE SANTIAGO

Spain, France, and Portugal

★☆☆☆☆

"They wouldn't let me cross the border just because my name was wrong on my passport."

TIMBUKTU

Timbuktu, Mali

★☆☆☆☆

*"Who said I should go here?
I don't remember who said to go."*

CHRIST THE REDEEMER

Rio de Janeiro, Brazil

"Can't say much. I never actually saw it."

CENOTE IK-KIL

Yucatán, Mexico

★☆☆☆☆

"You just bob in the water until you're ready to get out."

MOUNT EVEREST

Nepal

*"They don't let you drive up.
I tried."*

PYRAMIDS OF GIZA

Egypt

"My husband made me come here."

TAIPEI 101

*"I went 7 years ago and it basically didn't change at all.
Looked the same."*

AMAZON RIVER AND RAINFOREST

The Brazilian Amazon

"Just go to the Bahamas."

Quito, Ecuador

★☆☆☆☆

*"The real equator is a few meters away. So, this is fake.
Fake fake fake. It was a waste of time for my kids."*

MOUNT PINATUBO

Philippines

"This is for the person who wouldn't let us ride up on motorbikes: this mountain was here before you. It's not yours!"

CHANGING
OF THE GUARD

London, England

"The military band didn't play traditional music.
They played jazz and disco! They also played Grover
Washington Jr.'s 1980s hit 'Just The Two of Us.'"

SKELLIG MICHAEL

Ireland

"Had to go down the stairs on our behinds."

★☆☆☆☆

MACHU PICCHU

Peru

★☆☆☆☆

"Totally fake."

Ikoma, Tanzania

"The animals were rude."

STATUE OF LIBERTY

New York, USA

★☆☆☆☆

"Why is it green? Out of all the colours the person who created this beautiful lady could choose they went for green —if she was pink she'd get more attention. PERIOD."

THE SWISS ALPS

Switzerland

★☆☆☆☆

"I have not been this disappointed since I was 6 years old."

BURJ KHALIFA

Dubai, United Arab Emirates

"I didn't know where I was!"

CHARLES BRIDGE

Prague, Czech Republic

★☆☆☆☆

*"Cranky people ruin this city.
They would sigh when I talk."*

VERSAILLES

Paris, France

★☆☆☆☆

"There was NO KING or QUEEN. AM CONFUSED.
Did they die?"

ROUTE 66

USA

★☆☆☆☆

"Brian had a disagreement with a museum manager and we had to leave. This road was once the crown jewel of America!"

PARTHENON

Athens, Greece

"Keep your money and instead use it to get a massage and watch videos on YouTube about the Parthenon."

GRAND CANYON

Arizona, USA

★☆☆☆☆

"Cluster of ugly looking rocks. My pants were ripped."

NORTHERN LIGHTS

Lapland, Norway

★☆☆☆☆

*"I thought it would be WAY more colorful.
And it was TOO COLD."*

NEW ORLEANS GHOST TOUR

Louisiana, USA

★☆☆☆☆

*"We just walked around and talked about ghosts.
Did not see actual haunting."*

FUSHIMI INARI TAISHA

Kyoto, Japan

"My kids are totally bored. I had a good coffee."

★☆☆☆☆

JIGOKUDANI
SNOW MONKEY PARK

Japan

★☆☆☆☆

*"The monkeys are cute, but that's it.
Closed due to snow."*

ALCATRAZ

California, USA

★☆☆☆☆

"The woman that greeted us off the boat was BLAND and BORING."

REDWOOD NATIONAL PARK

California, USA

★☆☆☆☆

"I was sorely bummed."

GIANT'S CAUSEWAY

Northern Ireland

"The visitor center is soulless."

ST. PETER'S BASILICA

Vatican City

★☆☆☆☆

"Why do you have to pay to go into a church?"

STONEHENGE

Salisbury, England

"Could use a good cleaning and fresh paint."

TIANZI MOUNTAINS

China

★☆☆☆☆

"Only awesome if you like scenery."

MACLEAR'S BEACON

Cape Town, South Africa

★☆☆☆☆

"Friends, it was VERY boring."

THE DEAD SEA

"What am I doing?"

MONA LISA AT THE LOUVRE

Paris, France

★☆☆☆☆

"I saw someone being rude to a child who innocently was touching the art."

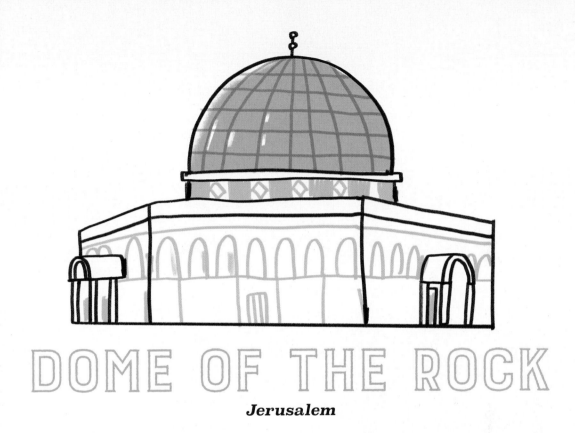

DOME OF THE ROCK

Jerusalem

*"We didn't get to see it.
Not the happiest moment on the trip."*

YELLOWSTONE NATIONAL PARK

Wyoming, USA

★☆☆☆☆

"The wifi was terrible."

TORRES DEL PAINE

Chilean Patagonia

"I think we went to the wrong place."

★☆☆☆☆

VENICE

Venice, Italy

★☆☆☆☆

"You will remember the smell of raw sewage."

OKTOBERFEST

Munich, Germany

"TOO MUCH SINGING. Lots of public drinking."

★☆☆☆☆

NEUSCHWANSTEIN CASTLE

Bavaria, Germany

★☆☆☆☆

"Parking was 10 euros. Biggest disappointment of my life."

GALÁPAGOS ISLANDS

Ecuador

"Did NOT appreciate my father getting yelled at for trying to touch a tortoise."

CINQUE TERRE

Liguria, Italy

★☆☆☆☆

"Recommended length of visit: 2 minutes."

WHITE CLIFFS OF DOVER

England, UK

"Our trip was cut short because my baby had to use the bathroom."

★☆☆☆☆

BRANDENBURG GATE

Berlin, Germany

⭐☆☆☆☆

"Just go to Rome instead. I really liked Rome. Rome will knock your socks off!"

MADAGASCAR

Madagascar, Africa

★☆☆☆☆

"Most overrated place on earth."

Athens, Greece

★☆☆☆☆

"Bathrooms not suitable for a dog."

ALHAMBRA

Granada, Spain

"There was a lot of security. And for what?
There was like nothing to steal!"

BIOLUMINESCENT MOSQUITO BAY

Vieques, Puerto Rico

"3 hours of my life I will never get back!"

VICTORIA FALLS

Livingstone, Zambia

"Too much water."

MIKE LOWERY is a *New York Times* bestselling illustrator and an author who has worked on more than eighty books for children and adults. He fell in love with travel as a kid, going on trips with his grandfather. As often as they can, he and his wife, Katrin, pack up their two kids and take them on an adventure. He draws in his sketchbook every day, and his travel drawings were collected in the book *Slightly Jet Lagged*. For some reason, he gets overly concerned about waterproof shoes before most of his trips.

He doesn't really travel with a backpack as shown in the drawing. He uses one of those suitcases with wheels because he's sort of older and worried about his back. He drew himself with a backpack because he thought it would make him look cooler.

This book is for Katrin, Allister, and Oskar,
my favorite people to see this planet with.